EXPLORING OUR UNIVERSE

PLANETS

LAUREN KUKLA

Checkerboard
Library

An Imprint of Abdo Publishing
abdopublishing.com

abdopublishing.com

Published by Abdo Publishing, a division of ABDO, PO Box 398166, Minneapolis, Minnesota 55439. Copyright ©2017 by Abdo Consulting Group, Inc. International copyrights reserved in all countries. No part of this book may be reproduced in any form without written permission from the publisher. Checkerboard Library™ is a trademark and logo of Abdo Publishing.
Printed in the United States of America, North Mankato, Minnesota
102016
012017

Design: Emily O'Malley, Mighty Media, Inc.
Production: Mighty Media, Inc.
Editor: Paige Polinsky
Cover Photograph: NASA
Interior Photographs: AP Images, p. 28; Getty Images, p. 13; Mighty Media, Inc., pp. 6, 7, 17, 19; NASA, pp. 9,
11 (top left and bottom right), 12, 16, 17 (top right), 18, 19, 21, 23, 25, 26; Shutterstock, p. 11 (top right);
Wikimedia Commons, pp. 11 (bottom left), 15 (top and bottom); Yuri Beletsky, p. 5

Publisher's Cataloging-in-Publication Data

Names: Kukla, Lauren, author.
Title: Planets / by Lauren Kukla.
Description: Minneapolis, MN : Abdo Publishing, 2017. | Series: Exploring our
    universe | Includes bibliographical references and index.
Identifiers: LCCN 2016944820 | ISBN 9781680784060 (lib. bdg.) |
    ISBN 9781680797596 (ebook)
Subjects: LCSH: Planets--Juvenile literature.
Classification: DDC 523.44--dc23
LC record available at http://lccn.loc.gov/2016944820

CONTENTS

MISSION
PLANETARY EXPLORATION

Have you ever looked up at the night sky? On a clear night, you can see thousands of lights. Most of these lights are stars. But if you're lucky, you might see a planet. Planets are often bigger and brighter than stars.

Our Home Planet

If you wanted to visit a planet, you wouldn't need to travel very far. In fact, you wouldn't need to travel at all! Earth is the planet we live on. It is also the only known planet that can support life.

Visiting Venus

Other planets are far away. Venus is usually the closest planet to Earth. In 2005, it took the *Venus Express* spacecraft five months to reach Venus from Earth.

In this photograph, the two brightest lights are the planets Jupiter (*left*) and Venus (*right*). They are much brighter than the stars around them.

A Long, Long Trip

It would take a long time to visit a planet outside our solar system. There, our nearest known planet orbits the star Alpha Centauri B. It would take more than 60,000 years to reach this planet in our fastest spacecraft!

5

CHAPTER 1

WHAT ARE PLANETS?

Planets are celestial bodies that orbit a star. An official planet must meet three requirements. First, it must be **spherical** in shape. Second, it must be large enough to have its own gravitational pull. And finally, it can't have any larger planets or objects in its orbit.

ALL ABOUT GRAVITY

Everything with mass has a gravitational pull, even you! The more mass an object has, the stronger its gravitational pull. The massive sun has a very powerful pull. It is strong

SUN

MERCURY   **VENUS**    **EARTH**    **MARS**   **JUPITER**

enough to attract all the planets in our solar system.

Planets have less mass than the stars they orbit. A planet's gravitational pull isn't strong enough to attract objects more massive than itself. But planets may attract moons, ice, dust, or other less massive objects. These become **satellites**. They orbit the planet.

Planets come in many sizes. Some are very big. Jupiter is the largest planet in our solar system. It is more than 1,000 times bigger than Earth. Mercury is the smallest planet in our solar system. It is about three times smaller than Earth.

SATURN

URANUS

NEPTUNE

CHAPTER 2

THE BIRTH OF A PLANET

To witness the birth of a planet, you would need to travel far back in time. In fact, you would have to go back to the birth of the planet's star. Earth's star, the sun, formed 4.5 billion years ago.

Like other stars, our sun began as a cloud of dust and gas. At the center of the cloud was a spinning **core**. As it spun, gravity caused this core to collapse. The gas and dust at the core became more compressed. As the core compressed, it grew very hot. Finally, the core became a glowing star.

The leftover gas and dust kept orbiting the new star. Over time, this material formed clumps that **collided** and stuck together. As these clumps grew bigger, they gained more gravitational pull. Some began attracting even more material, which added to their mass.

An artist's illustration of a new planet being formed. The star in the middle is surrounded by swirling gas, dust, and debris.

The force of the **collisions** caused the clumps to rotate. As they rotated, gravity pulled the material inward. This created a round shape. Eventually, these round clumps became the eight planets of our solar system.

CHAPTER 3

A HISTORY OF DISCOVERY

Ancient humans discovered five of our solar system's eight planets. They were Mercury, Venus, Mars, Jupiter, and Saturn. At first, people thought they were stars. Stars served many purposes at this time. Their movements allowed ancient people to navigate and track the seasons.

However, the ancients noticed that these five stars acted differently. They did not move in a consistent pattern. Instead, they appeared to wander across the sky. Ancient Greek astronomers named these strange stars *planets*, which means "wanderers."

These five planets were very important to ancient humans. Many people worshipped them as gods. In fact, most of our names for the planets come from the names of Greek and Roman gods. Uranus is named after the Greek god of the sky. Venus is the Roman goddess of love.

Mercury is the
Roman god of travel
and trickery.

Jupiter is the king
of the Roman gods.

In the 100s CE, Greek astronomer Ptolemy studied the planets. He thought they moved in a large orbit around Earth. For more than 1,000 years, most people believed Earth was the center of the universe.

Then, in the early 1500s, Polish astronomer Nicolaus Copernicus developed a new theory. He said

This map from the 1500s illustrates Ptolemy's idea of the universe. Earth is at the center, and the moon and sun are considered planets.

According to legend, Lippershey was inspired by watching his children play with glass lenses.

that all planets traveled around the sun. He also said Earth rotated on an axis, creating day and night.

Later astronomers improved Copernicus's theory, thanks to a new tool. In 1608, Dutch inventor Hans Lippershey created the first telescope. His invention quickly spread across Europe.

In 1609, Italian astronomer Galileo Galilei built his own telescope. He **confirmed** Copernicus's theory that the planets orbit the sun. He also discovered that, like the Earth, the sun rotates on an axis.

Meanwhile, German astronomer Johannes Kepler also studied planetary movement. His research supported Copernicus's theory that the planets orbit the sun. It also revealed that the planets' orbits are actually **elliptical**.

In the late 1600s and early 1700s, astronomers began to realize that the sun was not the center of the entire universe. Then, in 1781, British astronomer William Herschel discovered the planet Uranus. The planet Neptune was found in 1846.

SUPER SCIENTIST

JOHANNES KEPLER

Johannes Kepler was born in Germany on December 27, 1571. In 1589, he read about Copernicus's solar system theory. Kepler was determined to prove the theory correct. Using careful calculations, he developed three laws of planetary motion. These laws still hold true today. The first law states that the planets move in elliptical orbits. The other laws prove that a planet's orbiting speed is not constant. Instead, the planet moves faster when it is closer to the sun.

This map from the 1600s illustrates the Copernican universe. The Earth orbits around the sun.

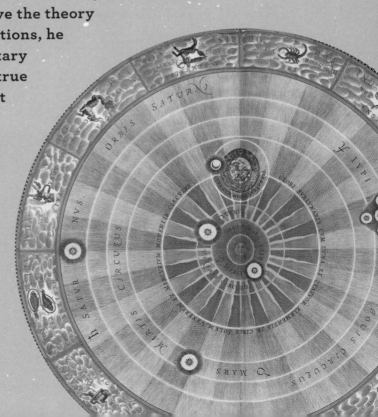

CHAPTER 4

OUR SOLAR SYSTEM

There are eight main planets in our solar system. Astronomers divide these planets into three groups. These groups are terrestrial planets, gas giants, and ice giants.

TERRESTRIAL PLANETS

Mercury, Venus, Earth, and Mars are the terrestrial planets. They are made mostly of rocks and metals. They also have fewer moons than the gas giants. Mercury is the closest planet to the sun. Temperatures there can reach 800 degrees Fahrenheit (427°C) during the day. However, this can drop to nearly −280 degrees Fahrenheit (−173°C) at night.

The "Blue Marble" is the first full-view photograph of Earth from space. It was taken in 1972 by the crew of Apollo 17.

Venus is the second planet from the sun. It is also the brightest planet. That is because sunlight reflects off its thick, poisonous atmosphere. The pressure of this atmosphere would crush a visiting human!

The next two planets are more **hospitable**. Earth is the only known place in the universe that supports life. Mars is the fourth planet. It is cold, dry, and dusty. However, scientists believe that Mars may have been warmer in the past. It may have even supported life!

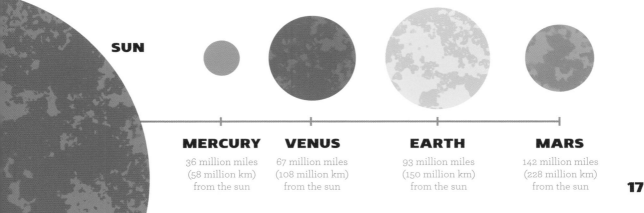

SUN

MERCURY	**VENUS**	**EARTH**	**MARS**
36 million miles (58 million km) from the sun	67 million miles (108 million km) from the sun	93 million miles (150 million km) from the sun	142 million miles (228 million km) from the sun

GAS GIANTS

Our solar system's final four planets are the gas giants. They are mostly made of the gases **hydrogen** and **helium**. The gas giants are much larger than the terrestrial planets. They also have more moons.

Jupiter is the largest gas giant. It is known for its stormy atmosphere. One storm, known as the Great Red Spot, is visible from Earth using telescopes. It has been raging for more than 300 years.

Gas giant Saturn is famous for its **complex** rings. These rings are made mostly of rock and ice. Some pieces are as large as buildings. Others are like grains of sand. Together, these pieces create a ring system about 175,000 miles (282,000 km) wide.

Jupiter's four largest moons are (top to bottom) Io, Europa, Ganymede, and Callisto.

Saturn's amazing ring system measures up to 300 feet (91 m) thick.

ICE GIANTS

Neptune and Uranus are the farthest planets from the sun. Uranus orbits on a tilted axis. This may be because a large object struck it at one time. Neptune is also **unique**. Its winds have been measured as being the fastest in the solar system. However, scientists do not know why.

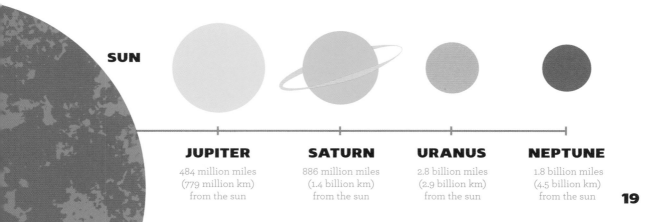

SUN

JUPITER	**SATURN**	**URANUS**	**NEPTUNE**
484 million miles (779 million km) from the sun	886 million miles (1.4 billion km) from the sun	2.8 billion miles (2.9 billion km) from the sun	1.8 billion miles (4.5 billion km) from the sun

CHAPTER 5

DWARF PLANETS

In 1930, astronomer Clyde W. Tombaugh spotted a faraway speck of light through a telescope. This led to the discovery of an icy ninth planet, Pluto. But in 2003, an astronomer spotted an object beyond Pluto. This object was larger than Pluto. It was named Eris.

Astronomers then questioned whether Pluto was a real planet. Pluto was much smaller than the other planets. It also had other large objects in its orbit. So, in 2006, astronomers declared Pluto a dwarf planet.

DID YOU KNOW ?

Pluto was discovered by mistake. Astronomers found that Neptune and Uranus had wobbly orbits. They thought an unknown planet was causing the wobble. Tombaugh started looking for this planet and found Pluto. Later measurements revealed the original wobble had been a math error!

Dwarf planets must meet two requirements. First, they must have enough mass to be nearly round. Second, they must orbit the sun in a regular pattern. Unlike regular planets, dwarf planets have other objects in their orbits. Today, astronomers know of five dwarf planets, including Pluto and Eris. But many more are likely waiting to be discovered.

21

CHAPTER 6

EXOPLANETS

In 1992, scientists announced the discovery of two new planets. These special planets, called exoplanets, are outside our solar system. The two small rocky worlds orbit a star in the constellation Virgo.

Three years later, scientists discovered another exoplanet. This planet is 50 **light-years** away. It orbits a sun-like star in the constellation Pegasus. Since the 1990s, we have found more than 1,000 exoplanets. And new discoveries keep coming!

Astronomers want to find exoplanets able to support life. So, they look for planets about the size of Earth. These exoplanets must be close enough to their stars to have liquid water. However, they must not to be too hot. This ideal distance is known as the **habitable** zone. Several planets have been discovered in this zone.

Kepler-186f is an exoplanet discovered in 2014. It is the first known earth-size planet existing in the habitable zone.

CHAPTER 7

EXPLORING PLANETS

Most exoplanets are too far away to see. So, astronomers look for clues given off by an exoplanet's star. For example, if a star's light dims, that means a planet may be passing in front of it. Astronomers measure how much light the object blocks. This data helps estimate its size.

Astronomers measure a star's wobble to find planets. As a planet orbits a star, its gravitational pull makes the star wobble. Astronomers may notice a regular wobble on a distant star. That is a sign a planet orbits it.

In our own solar system, astronomers use tools such as **probes** to study planets. Probes fly past planets, sending data back to astronomers. The first successful probes were launched in 1958. Since then, probes have provided valuable information about our planets. Some have traveled to the very edges of our solar system.

TOOLS OF DISCOVERY

KEPLER

In 2009, NASA launched a satellite with a huge mission. *Kepler*, named after Johannes Kepler, would scan the Milky Way galaxy. It would send exoplanet data back to scientists. By 2015, *Kepler* had identified more than 4,000 possible exoplanets. However, only 1,000 were confirmed by scientists.

NASA's *Kepler* fuels up at an Astrotech facility in Titusville, Florida.

NASA's car-sized *Curiosity* takes a self-portrait on
Mars. *Curiosity* arrived on the red planet in 2012.

Humans have yet to land on a planet other than Earth.
But scientists have sent robots to explore Mars. In 1971,
the Soviet Union successfully landed **probes** on Mars.
It was the first country to do so. The probes stopped

working shortly after landing. But they still provided a lot of data.

In 2003, **NASA** landed two **rovers** on Mars. Their goal was to travel slowly across Mars's surface. The rovers studied rocks and looked for signs of liquid water or simple life-forms. One rover traveled 4.8 miles (7.7 km) before getting stuck. The other has traveled 26.48 miles (42.6 km) so far and is still going.

NASA hopes to send astronauts to Mars in the future. But it won't be easy. Their spacecraft will need to carry enough fuel to return home. Meanwhile, private companies are also planning journeys to Mars. Mars One, a nonprofit foundation, plans to send a crew there in 2026. It will be a one-way trip.

No one knows what new planetary discoveries are coming. Will astronomers find life on a faraway exoplanet? Will humans colonize Mars? No matter where planetary exploration takes us, it is sure to lead to amazing discoveries.

PLANETARY GUIDEBOOK

Mercury
- About 36 million miles (58 million km) from the sun
- Year Length: 88 Earth days
- Known Moons: 0

Venus
- About 67 million miles (108 million km) from the sun
- Year Length: 225 Earth days
- Known Moons: 0

Earth
- About 93 million miles (150 million km) from the sun
- Year Length: 365.26 Earth days
- Known Moons: 1

An illustration of the future Mars One colony. The foundation plans on sending four astronauts to Mars every two years.

Mars

- About 142 million miles (228 million km) from the sun
- Year Length: 687 Earth days
- Known Moons: 2

Jupiter

- About 484 million miles (779 million km) from the sun
- Year Length: 12 Earth years
- Known Moons: 62

Saturn

- About 886 million miles (1.4 billion km) from the sun
- Year Length: 29 Earth years
- Known Moons: 53

DID YOU KNOW ?

The farther a planet is from the sun, the longer its year lasts!

Uranus

- About 1.8 billion miles (2.9 billion km) from the sun
- Year Length: 84 Earth years
- Known Moons: 27

Neptune

- About 2.8 billion miles (4.5 billion km) from the sun
- Year Length: 165 Earth years
- Known Moons: 13

GLOSSARY

collide — to come together with force. An act or instance of colliding is a collision.

complex — having many parts, details, ideas, or functions.

confirm — to say that something is definitely true or will definitely happen, when it was previously just a rumor or a possibility.

core — the central part of a celestial body, usually having different physical properties from the surrounding parts.

elliptical — having a flat oval shape.

galaxy — a very large group of stars and planets.

habitable — safe and good enough for people to live in.

helium — a light, colorless gas that does not burn.

hospitable — having an environment where plants, animals, or people can live or grow easily.

hydrogen — a gas with no smell or color that is lighter than air and catches fire easily.

light-year — the distance that light travels in one year.

NASA — National Aeronautics and Space Administration. NASA is a US government agency that manages the nation's space program and conducts flight research.

probe — a device used to explore and send back information.

rover — a vehicle used for exploring the surface of space objects.

satellite — an object, either natural or manufactured, that orbits a larger heavenly body. A manufactured satellite relays scientific information back to Earth.

spherical (SFIHR-i-kuhl) — having a globe-shaped body.

unique (yoo-NEEK) — being the only one of its kind.

WEBSITES

To learn more about Exploring Our Universe, visit booklinks.abdopublishing.com. These links are routinely monitored and updated to provide the most current information available.

INDEX